FUN with FOOD WEBS

FOREST FOOD WEBS

Written by Charis Mather

KidHaven PUBLISHING

Published in 2024 by
KidHaven Publishing, an Imprint of Greenhaven Publishing, LLC
2544 Clinton St., Buffalo, NY 14224

Written by: Charis Mather
Edited by: Rebecca Phillips-Bartlett
Designed by: Dan Scase

Image Credits
All images are courtesy of Shutterstock.com, unless otherwise specified—with thanks to Getty Images, Thinkstock Photo, and iStockphoto. Cover – Funny Solution Studio, Pim Leijen, FotograFFF, Rob Jansen, Edwin Godinho, TSN52. 4–5 – Natalia Golubnycha, PNPImages. 6–7 – PNPImages, AB Photographie, Lisa Hagan, Giedriius, Debbie Steinhausser, adamikarl, Mila_22 79. 8–9 – Don Mammoser , PeopleImages.com - Yuri A. 10–11 – FrentaN, Mila_22 79. 12–13 – Warren Metcalf, Sergey Uryadnikov, Rudmer Zwerver, adamikarl. 14–15 – DejaVuDesigns, Debbie Steinhausser. 16–17 – Giedriius. 18–19 – AB Photographie, Alessandro Cancian. 20–21 – Carol Gray , Lisa Hagan. 22–23 – FotoRequest, Joe McDonald, AB Photographie, Lisa Hagan, Warren Metcalf, Giedriius, Debbie Steinhausser, adamikarl, Mila_22 79, FrentaN.

Cataloging-in-Publication Data

Names: Mather, Charis, 1999-.
Title: Forest food webs / Charis Mather.
Description: Buffalo, New York: KidHaven Publishing, 2024. |
Series: Fun with food webs | Includes glossary and index.
Identifiers: ISBN 9781534546059 (pbk.) | ISBN 9781534546066 (library bound) |
ISBN 9781534546073 (ebook)
Subjects: LCSH: Forest ecology--Juvenile literature. | Forest animals--Juvenile literature. |
Food chains (Ecology)--Juvenile literature.
Classification: LCC QH541.5.F6 M38 2024 | DDC 577.3--dc23

Manufactured in the United States of America

CPSIA compliance information: Batch #CW24KH: For further information contact Greenhaven Publishing LLC at 1-844-317-7404.

Please visit our website, www.greenhavenpublishing.com.
For a free color catalog of all our high-quality books, call toll free 1-844-317-7404 or fax 1-844-317-7405.

Find us on

CONTENTS

Words that look like ***THIS*** can be found in the glossary on page 24.

THE FOREST ECOSYSTEM

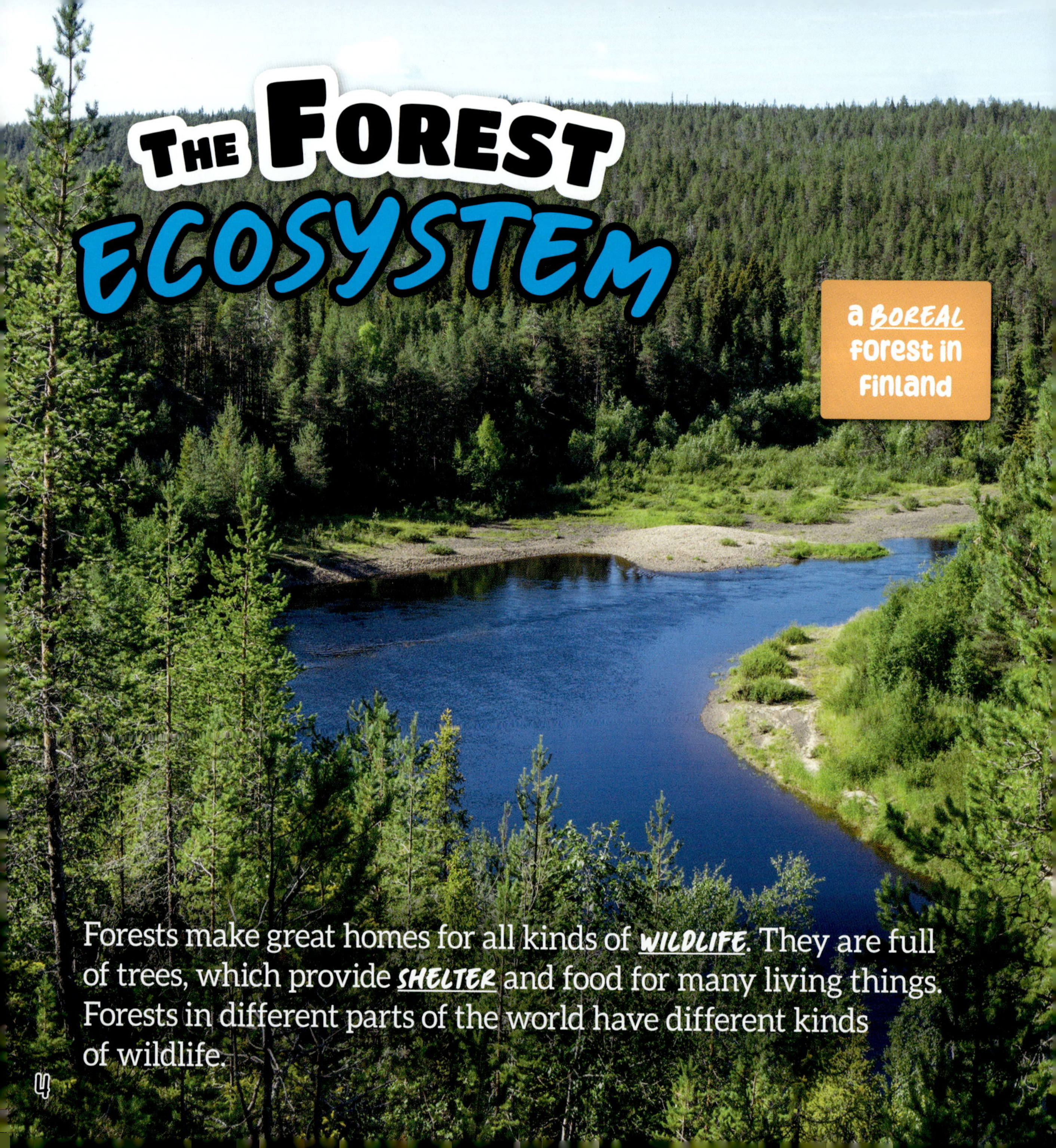

a ***BOREAL*** forest in Finland

Forests make great homes for all kinds of ***WILDLIFE***. They are full of trees, which provide ***SHELTER*** and food for many living things. Forests in different parts of the world have different kinds of wildlife.

The living things in a forest, as well as all the nonliving things around them, make up a forest **ECOSYSTEM**. Each living thing in the ecosystem needs other living things to survive.

Food Chains and Food Webs

Each living things has its own role, or part, in an ecosystem. Some living things become food for other creatures. Food chains show which living things are food for other living things.

a boreal forest food chain

Forests have many different types of wildlife, so there are many food chains in this ecosystem. When food chains overlap and connect, they make a food web.

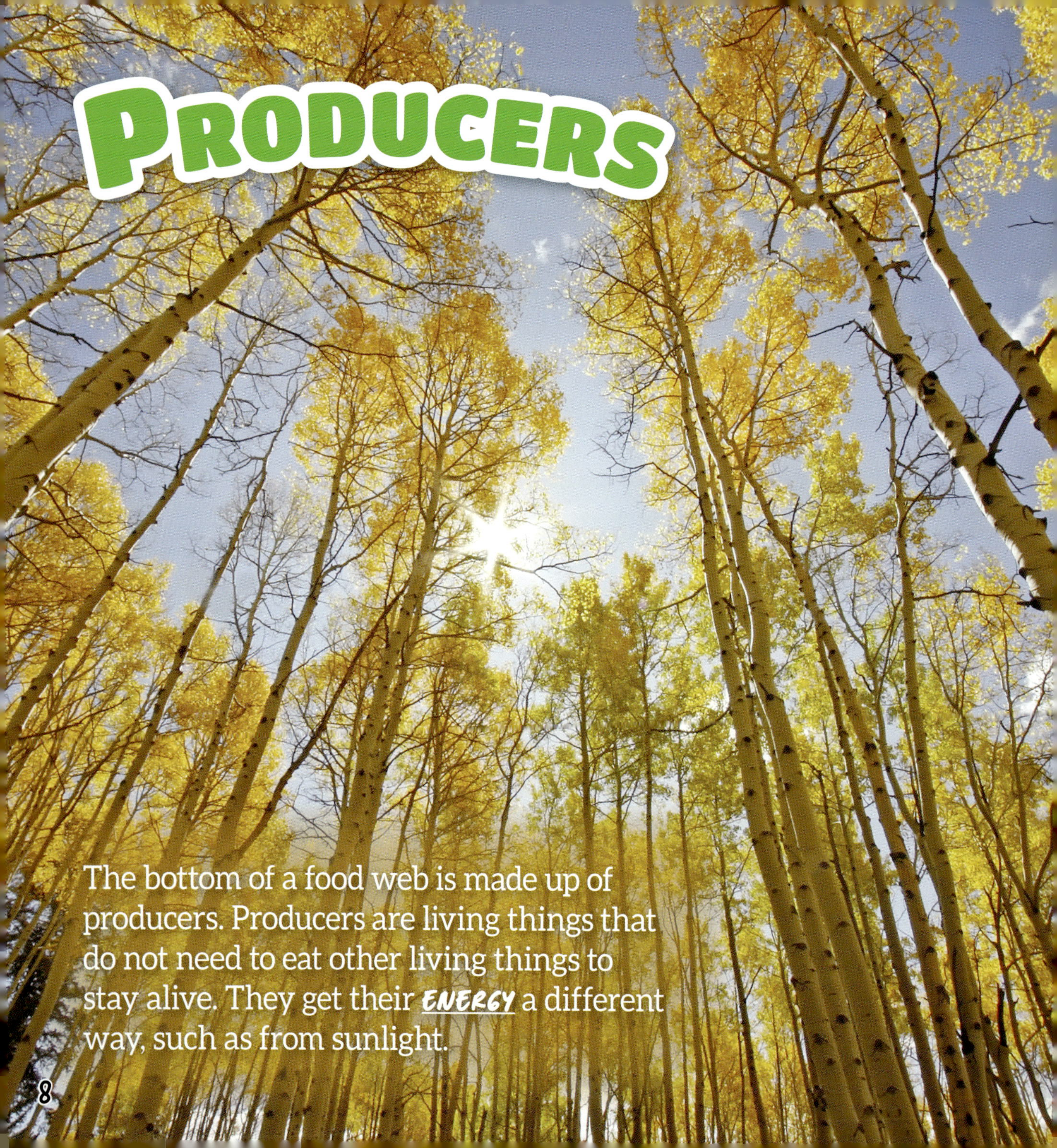

PRODUCERS

The bottom of a food web is made up of producers. Producers are living things that do not need to eat other living things to stay alive. They get their ***ENERGY*** a different way, such as from sunlight.

Producers do not eat other living things, but other living things will eat them. They are food for animals higher up in the food web. Plants are the most common type of producer.

White Birch Trees

Food: made with energy from the sun

Eaten by: deer, squirrels, mice, snowshoe hares

Forests are filled with trees, which are a kind of producer. Forests in warmer places may have different kinds of trees than forests in colder places. White birch trees can be found in cooler areas.

Dwarf Shrubs

There are other producers in forests besides trees. Some forests have many dwarf shrubs. Dwarf shrubs are small, woody bushes. Their leaves, twigs, and berries are food for many creatures higher up in the food web.

Food: made with energy from the sun

Eaten by: deer, squirrels, mice, snowshoe hares, skunks, red foxes

CONSUMERS

Animals that eat other living things are consumers. Plant-eating consumers are called herbivores. Meat eaters are carnivores. Animals that eat plants and meat are omnivores. Consumers are higher up in food webs than producers.

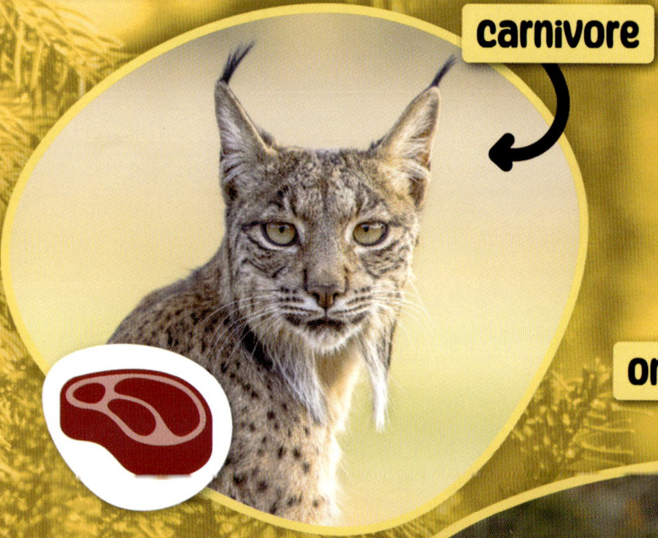

Squirrels

Food: white birch, dwarf shrubs, nuts, insects, bird eggs

Eaten by: great horned owls, red foxes, gray wolves, skunks

Squirrels are small ***rodents*** with bushy tails. Squirrels eat many different plants. They are omnivores, so they will also eat insects and eggs from birds. Squirrels are eaten by many forest ***predators***.

Skunks

Skunks are nocturnal animals, which means they mostly come out at night. Skunks look for plants to eat or hunt small animals, such as mice and squirrels.

FOOD:
dwarf shrubs, mice, ground squirrels, insects, bird eggs

EATEN BY:
great horned owls, red foxes, gray wolves

Skunks have some predators, but they know how to keep them away. When skunks feel they are in danger, they lift their tail and aim a stinky spray at the predators!

Red Foxes

Like skunks, red foxes are more active at night. However, this means they have to watch out for other nocturnal predators, such as owls.

Food: skunks, mice, squirrels, hares, dwarf shrubs, bird eggs

Eaten by: great horned owls, bears, coyotes

Foxes are great hunters, but they also eat plants. Foxes eat berries from dwarf shrubs, especially in the summer. In the winter, they may eat more meat.

Apex Predators

The animals at the very top of a food web are called apex predators. Apex predators are consumers that are generally not eaten by other animals in their ecosystem.

Gray Wolves

Food:	**Eaten by:**
deer, mice, skunks, squirrels, snowshoe hares	no one

Gray wolves are one of the top predators in the forest food web. These carnivores mostly hunt big animals, such as deer. However, they may also hunt smaller animals, such as mice and squirrels.

Great Horned Owls

At night, animals in the forest have to watch out for great horned owls. These large birds can silently swoop down on their **prey** and grab them with their long claws.

Great horned owls eat many different kinds of animals. If their prey is small enough, they may swallow their food whole. Larger prey may be carried off to their nests to be eaten more slowly.

Food: mice, squirrels, skunks, red foxes, snowshoe hares

Eaten by: no one

A Forest Food Web

This food web shows how energy moves through a forest ecosystem. Start with the sun and the producers at the bottom, and follow the arrows to see what is eaten by what.

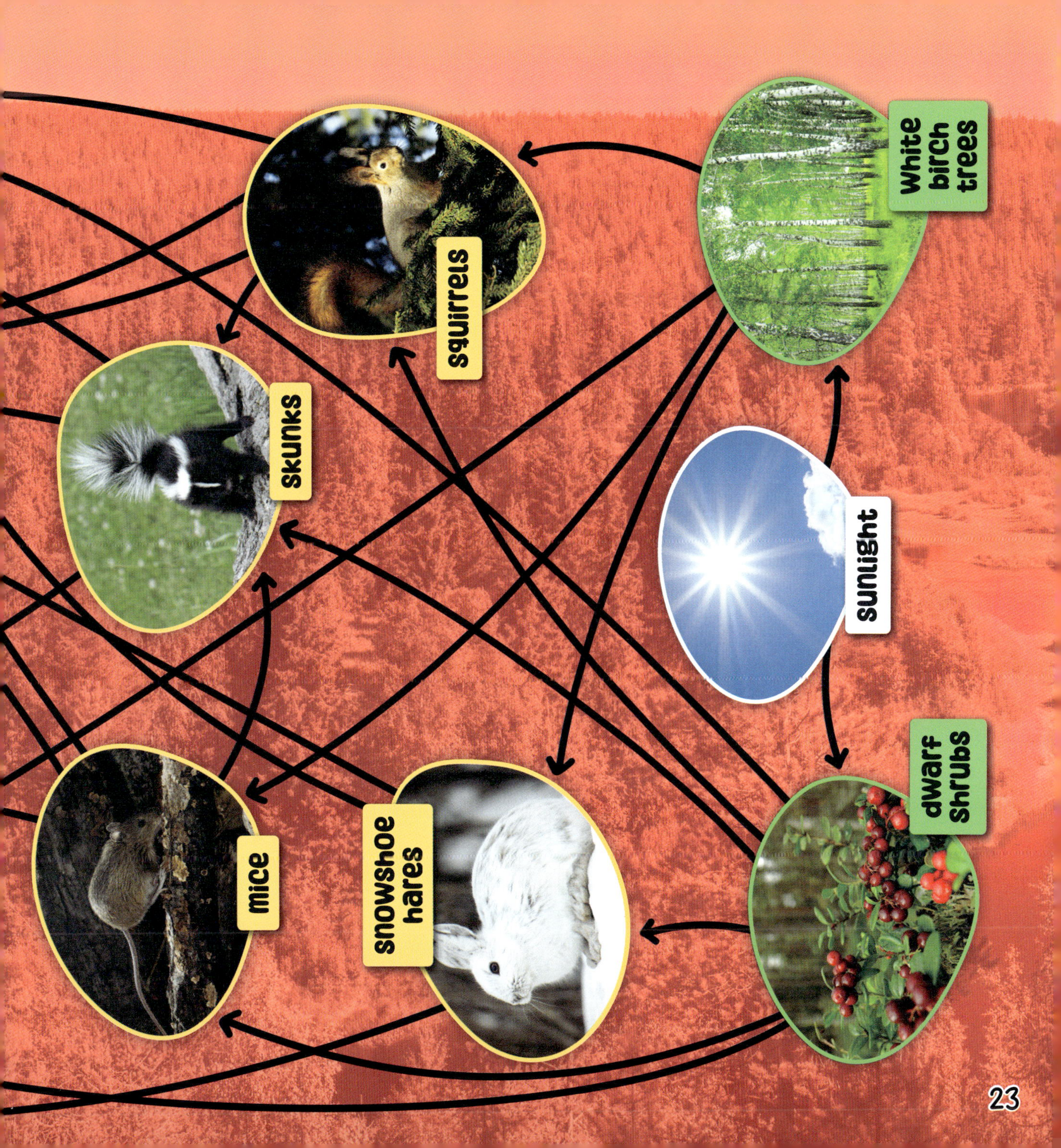
White birch trees
squirrels
skunks
sunlight
dwarf shrubs
snowshoe hares
mice

GLOSSARY

boreal	describing a type of forest that is found in colder areas in the north
ecosystem	a community of living things and the environment they live in
energy	the power and ability to do work
predators	animals that hunt other animals for food
prey	animals that are eaten by other animals for food
rodents	mammals, such as mice, rats, and squirrels, that have long front teeth that grow throughout their whole lives
shelter	a safe place to stay
wildlife	the animals, and sometimes plants, that live in an area

INDEX